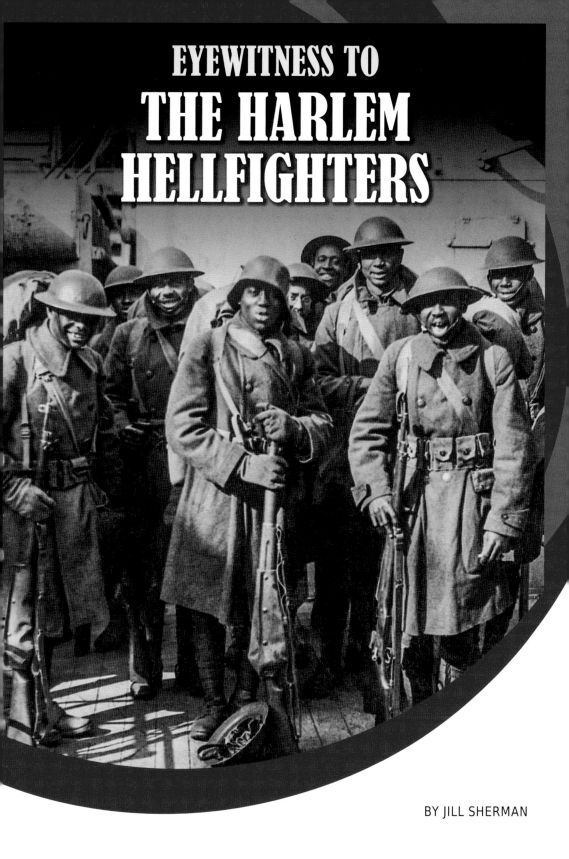

EYEWITNESS TO
THE HARLEM
HELLFIGHTERS

BY JILL SHERMAN

Published by The Child's World®
1980 Lookout Drive • Mankato, MN 56003-1705
800-599-READ • www.childsworld.com

Photographs ©: U.S. National Archives and Records Administration, cover, 1, 5, 6, 9, 11, 14, 24; Library of Congress, 10; Everett Historical/Shutterstock Images, 12, 15; The Print Collector Heritage Images/Newscom, 16; U.S. Army, 19; The City College of New York, 20; Bettmann/Getty Images, 22, 27; Underwood Archives/UIG Universal Images Group/Newscom, 23; Lisa Ferdinando, 28

ISBN 9781503816046

LCCN 2016945612

Printed in the United States of America
PA02317

ABOUT THE AUTHOR

Jill Sherman lives and writes in Brooklyn, New York. She has written more than a dozen books for young readers. She enjoys researching new topics and believes it is important to remember the past so that we can be sympathetic to those who have suffered and continue to do better in the future.

TABLE OF
CONTENTS

FAST FACTS

Who were the Harlem Hellfighters?

- The Harlem Hellfighters started as part of the New York 15th National Guard Unit.
- They formed the all-black 369th Infantry Regiment during World War I (1914–1918).
- They earned the nickname "Harlem Hellfighters" for their actions in battle.

How were the Hellfighters treated?

- U.S. leaders decided to **segregate** the military. Black soldiers were often treated worse than white soldiers.
- Some U.S. military leaders blamed the 369th for shortcomings in battle. Five Hellfighters faced charges and were tried by a military court.

What did the Hellfighters accomplish in battle?

- The 369th saw more combat than any other regiment.
- The Hellfighters served bravely in the Meuse-Argonne offensive.

How are the Hellfighters remembered?

- The 369th was honored with a parade when it returned to New York City.

- The French awarded members with the Croix de Guerre. The medal is the country's highest military award.

- The U.S. government awarded Hellfighter Henry Johnson with the Purple Heart and Medal of Honor after his death.

Chapter 1

JOINING UP

In the spring of 1917, young, black Virginian farmer Charles Brodnax signed his name to the **draft** list. The United States had just joined the **Allied** countries in World War I. U.S. president Woodrow Wilson had called for young men to sign up for military service. "The world must be made safe for **democracy**," Wilson had said.[1]

◄ **U.S. secretary of war Newton Baker picks out a number during the draft. The numbers indicated who would be drafted.**

Many Americans, including Brodnax, answered the president's call. They believed it was their duty to protect democracy. But for some black Americans, the decision did not come so easily.

Brodnax had heard the arguments against enlisting. Newspapers printed stories pointing out Wilson's **hypocrisy**. The articles stated that black Americans had no duty to protect democracy when they were being blocked from voting in many states. The *Baltimore Afro-American* asked, "Will someone tell us just how long Mr. Wilson has been a convert to true democracy?"[2]

Despite the criticisms, Brodnax decided to join the 2.3 million black Americans who signed up for the draft.

> "Let us, while this war lasts . . . close our ranks shoulder to shoulder with our white fellow citizens and the allied nations that are fighting for democracy."
>
> *—W. E. B. Du Bois, U.S. civil rights leader, in support of black soldiers fighting in World War I*[3]

"I felt that I belonged to the government of my country and should answer to the call and obey the orders in defense of democracy," Brodnax said.[4]

When Brodnax signed up for service, he knew black soldiers would face challenges. One of those challenges had to do with the problem of **hierarchy**. The U.S. Army follows a strict chain of command. Officers expect to be treated with respect. Low-ranking soldiers address high-ranking officers as "sir." Southern politicians argued for segregation in the army. They said it could cause problems if a white soldier had to call a black soldier "sir." The politicians thought it would change the country's racial balance.

Wilson agreed to segregate the army. Brodnax joined the all-black 15th New York National Guard Unit. Then, in July 1917, Wilson brought the 15th National Guard into national service. Brodnax went into service as part of the U.S. Army.

Brodnax and the 15th went to train in Spartanburg, South Carolina. As was the case in many states, South Carolina had a history of racial tension. The state had left the United States during the Civil War (1861–1865) over the issue of slavery.

In addition, violence had recently broken out between white and black people in cities across the United States.

▲ **Members of the New York 15th National Guard stand at attention.**

Tension between white and black workers in East Saint Louis, Illinois, ended in riots. More than 100 black people were killed.

Members of the 15th were met with hostility in South Carolina. Sometimes when trainees walked around in their military uniforms, white people pushed them off the sidewalks. Other white civilians shouted insults at the soldiers.

▲ Black protesters silently march in response to violence against black citizens in East Saint Louis.

Members of the 15th also faced hostility at training camp. White officers had low expectations for the black recruits. Some wrongfully believed black people were lazy and unintelligent. Members of the 15th kept quiet. They focused on training.

They went through drills, learned military procedures, and practiced firing their weapons. The 15th left Spartanburg without incident. They had proven themselves. They were headed to Europe as the 369th Infantry Regiment of the U.S. Army.

▲ **Black troops aboard the USS *Louisville* travel to fight in France.**

Chapter 2

BLACK SOLDIERS AT WAR

The men of the 369th stepped onto the beaches of France on January 1, 1918. Soon they were on their way to the front lines. The long, heavy march toward the fight was hard work. As they marched, they passed blind men, sick men, and men missing limbs. One member of the 369th asked an approaching soldier where all the wounded were coming from.

"They're coming from right where you're going the day after tomorrow," the officer said.[5]

But as black regiments arrived in France, so did a message from the U.S. military. General John J. Pershing was the commander of U.S. troops overseas. At the beginning of the war, Pershing had refused to supply U.S. soldiers to the French and British armies. Pershing wanted U.S. soldiers to fight together under U.S. leadership. But now some all-black regiments, including the 369th, were being sent to join the French forces.

"Everywhere the offensive spirit is alive, pulsating, waiting for the hour to strike, that the spirit of real and true democracy will not perish."

—Osceola McKaine, 367th Infantry, an all-black regiment[7]

Opening the message, French officers read the U.S. military's instructions. "We must prevent the rise of any pronounced degree of intimacy between French officers and black officers," the message said.[6]

▲ **Black and white soldiers line up for food in Toulouse, France.**

The message went on to advise against shaking hands with black soldiers, eating with them, or praising them for their work. The guidelines given in the message were similar to laws that enforced segregation in the United States. The U.S. military hoped the French would adopt the rules. The French officers scoffed at the U.S. military's instructions. They burned the message.

Black soldiers did not have to wait long to be sent into battle. They faced many horrors common to the front lines. They dodged artillery strikes, machine-gun fire, and gas attacks.

"Flashes of fire, the metallic crack of high explosives, the awful explosions that dug holes fifteen and twenty feet [5–6 m] in diameter," were among the images U.S. major Warner Ross recalled.[8] While at camp, rats ran across the soldiers' bunks. Lice nested in soldiers' hair.

Despite the difficult conditions, black soldiers acted bravely in battle. No soldier displayed this more than one of the shining heroes of World War I: Henry Johnson.

▲ **Members of the 369th stand at ready in the trenches of France on May 4, 1918.**

Chapter 3

WAR HERO

In the early hours on May 15, 1918, Henry Johnson and Needham Roberts of the 369th were standing guard. The soldiers had recently arrived on France's western front. The 369th was under French command. Few members of the 369th spoke French. But they understood enough to follow their orders. Johnson and Roberts had been assigned to **sentry** duty. They kept watch while other soldiers slept.

◀ Soldiers on the front lines cut through a tangle of barbed wire.

Sentry duty was often uneventful. But this time, in the dead of night, Roberts heard a sound. *Click*. Then another. *Click*. In the darkness, someone was snipping apart barbed wire. The barbed wire was a barrier between the Allied and German front lines.

Roberts and Johnson took cover in their **dugout**. They got ready for an attack by German soldiers. Johnson and Roberts lined up their grenades. As soon as the Germans crossed the Allied line, the two Americans started their attack.

The Germans responded. German grenades showered **shrapnel** down on Johnson and Roberts. A blast threw Roberts back against a wall. He was badly hurt and bleeding from the shoulder and hip. Unable to stand, Roberts passed grenades to Johnson. Johnson threw them toward the German attackers.

Roberts shouted for help. But as the Germans pushed forward, Johnson alone was around to fight off the attack. Johnson grabbed his rifle. But he mistakenly put French shells into his U.S. rifle. It jammed. Unable to shoot, Johnson turned his rifle around. He swung it as a club. The weapon crashed down on a German soldier's head. The rifle broke from the force. More Germans entered the dugout. Johnson grabbed his knife and continued to fight them off. He slashed quickly and powerfully.

17

Johnson's attack frightened the German soldiers. And as the French and U.S. soldiers approached, the Germans ran away. Johnson moved over to check on Roberts. Together they walked away from the dugout. Exhausted and hurt badly, Johnson collapsed.

> "There wasn't anything so fine about it—just fought for my life. A rabbit would have done that."
>
> —Henry Johnson, on fighting off the German raid[9]

By daylight, the proof of Johnson's heroics was clear. Four German soldiers lay at the site of the attack. Items left behind by the retreating soldiers were scattered about. Based on the equipment left behind, officers estimated Johnson fought off 20 German soldiers. He had saved Roberts and potentially many more French and U.S. soldiers. But Johnson had suffered 21 wounds. He had taken bullets to the head and the lip. Bones in his left foot were broken. At a nearby hospital, doctors tended to Johnson's injuries.

The French military honored Johnson and Roberts for their actions. All French forces in the area attended the ceremony.

Johnson and Roberts stood proudly as they were awarded cross medals. They were the first Americans to receive the Croix de Guerre. It is the highest honor the French military can give to a soldier.

▲ **Henry Johnson poses with his Croix de Guerre in February 1919.**

Chapter 4

MEUSE-ARGONNE OFFENSIVE

In September 1918, French and U.S. troops marched again. Among them was Horace Pippin of the 369th. Little did Pippin and the other men know they were about to enter the most important battle of the war. General Pershing had planned a powerful attack. He sent U.S. and French armies to the Meuse River and the Argonne Forest. Pershing's plan was bold.

With a strong attack, he hoped to cut off the entire German 2nd Army.

At daybreak on September 26, 1918, Pershing ordered the Allies to attack. Pippin and the 369th flooded the battlefield. Approximately 700 Allied tanks rolled ahead. The Allies pressed forward toward the German lines.

But Pershing had underestimated the German's fighting power. German machine guns cut down U.S. and French soldiers. Pershing scrambled to come up with a plan.

Luckily, the 369th had managed to fight their way forward. Pippin and his fellow soldiers moved up under heavy fire. German machine gunners and snipers seemed to be shooting from every angle. Still, through hot and smoking shell holes, the 369th pressed ahead. Pippin and the 369th attacked with such fierceness the Germans created a nickname for them. They called them "Hellfighters."[10]

Word of the Hellfighters spread quickly. The word "Harlem" was soon added to their nickname. Harlem is a historically black part of New York City, where many of the soldiers of the 369th were from. Despite the Harlem Hellfighters' success, the Meuse-Argonne offensive dragged on for more than a month.

▲ Soldiers show off their Croix de Guerre medals following the Meuse-Argonne offensive.

The fighting finally stopped on November 11, 1918. Leaders from both sides signed an agreement on that day, ending all combat. The 369th was coming home.

French general Georges Lebouc praised the Hellfighters. He said the men "sacrificed without regard for themselves."[11] Lebouc honored 171 Hellfighters with the Croix de Guerre. But not everyone saw the Hellfighters' actions in the same way. Many of the soldiers at the Meuse-Argonne offensive were unprepared for the fierce battle. A number of soldiers, both black and white, **deserted**. But black soldiers took much of the blame. Five black officers were put on trial.

U.S. colonel William Hayward criticized the men harshly. In a message to the president, Hayward wrote, "To the disgrace of the regiment . . . large numbers of enlisted men of their regiment conducted themselves in the most cowardly and disgraceful manner."[12] In his letter, he asked for punishment for those who deserted, including executions. The U.S. military was embarrassed by the offensive's slow progress. Officers such as Hayward wanted a group to blame for the failures. Many chose to blame the soldiers of the 369th because they were black.

▲ **Colonel William Hayward (right) was critical of the soldiers from the 369th.**

Chapter 5

HOMECOMING

On the cold morning of February 17, 1919, New Yorkers of all colors crowded along Fifth Avenue. Though they covered themselves with shawls and blankets against the morning cold, they grinned proudly. They were excited to see New York's own heroes. The 369th Infantry Regiment, the Harlem Hellfighters, had returned from war.

◀ **New Yorkers line the streets to welcome home the Harlem Hellfighters.**

The 369th was the first full regiment to return to the United States. New York City threw a parade to celebrate. The 369th was returning as the most awarded regiment in the U.S. Army. Schools in Harlem did not hold classes that day. Students were free to welcome the hero regiment home. As the Hellfighters came into view, the crowd of more than 250,000 cheered. The cheer drowned out the music of the marching band.

To those watching, the soldiers seemed to be larger than life. These men had spent more time in combat than any other U.S. unit. They had never given up a trench or lost a man to capture. Each soldier wore a gold stripe on one sleeve, indicating one year of service. On the opposite sleeve, many soldiers had more stripes. These marked their battle wounds.

Bringing up the rear was Henry Johnson. He rode in an open car with other injured soldiers. Johnson joyfully waved to the crowd. A steel plate held Johnson's injured foot together. Despite the pain, he stood up and greeted the crowd.

After the homecoming events, Johnson and the Harlem Hellfighters were quickly forgotten. Racial tension was at a high point in the United States. That summer became known as the Red Summer of 1919 because of the racial violence that occurred.

> "Henry Johnson . . . displayed the most profound battlefield bravery in World War I, yet the nation for which he was willing to give his life shamefully failed to recognize his heroics, just because he was a black man."
>
> —*New York senator Charles E. Schumer, on June 2, 2015*[13]

Riots erupted in cities in the North and the South. In one case, a black boy was caught swimming on a white beach in Chicago, Illinois. White men approached him. The men told him he was not wanted there because he was black. A fight broke out. During the fight, a young black man drowned. Police officers arrived on the scene. They refused to arrest any of the white men who had caused the young man's death. Instead, the black men involved in the fight were taken away. Angry citizens continued the fight in the city streets. White and black people threw stones at each other.

Similar events in other cities led to massacres that affected thousands of black families. The democracy the Hellfighters had fought for seemed further away than ever.

Police escort a man to safety during riots in Chicago, Illinois, ▶ in 1919.

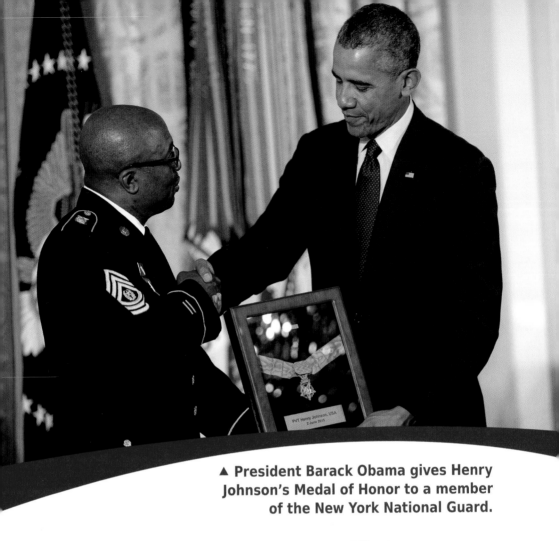

▲ President Barack Obama gives Henry
Johnson's Medal of Honor to a member
of the New York National Guard.

The Hellfighters themselves faced great difficulties getting
their military benefits. Johnson, in particular, had a hard time.
Johnson read through his **discharge** papers. He saw they did
not mention that he had been wounded. The injuries made
it difficult for Johnson to work. His health got worse. All but
forgotten by the country he had fought to protect, Johnson died
in 1929. Johnson received no honors from the U.S. military during
his lifetime.

It took many years before Johnson was honored by his own country's government. In 1996 U.S. president Bill Clinton awarded Johnson the Purple Heart. The Purple Heart is given to soldiers injured or killed in battle. In 2001 Johnson was awarded the Distinguished Service Cross. It is the U.S. military's second-highest honor. Finally, in 2015, President Barack Obama awarded Johnson the Medal of Honor, the U.S. military's highest honor. It was 97 years after he had served. Standing in front of military service men and women, Obama spoke about Johnson's accomplishments. The crowd applauded as the president handed the medal to a member of the New York National Guard.

THINK ABOUT IT

- Why did Wilson decide to allow black soldiers to enlist in the U.S. military?
- Imagine you were a black soldier who fought for the United States in World War I. What might it feel like to be blamed for the military's failures in the war?
- Why did it take so long for the United States to honor Johnson's service with the Purple Heart and Medal of Honor?

GLOSSARY

Allied (AL-ide): Allied countries were those that fought together against Germany and other countries in World War I. The United States and United Kingdom were two Allied countries.

democracy (di-MAH-kruh-see): Democracy is a system of government in which people choose their leaders by voting. The United States has a democracy.

deserted (di-ZUR-tid): To have deserted is to have ended one's military service without justification. Untrained soldiers deserted during the Meuse-Argonne offensive.

discharge (DIS-charj): To discharge is to release someone from a term of duty. Discharge papers released a soldier from military service.

draft (DRAFT): The draft was a system that required young men to serve in the military. Young men were required to sign up for the draft.

dugout (DUHG-out): A dugout is an underground shelter. Soldiers on sentry duty kept watch from a dugout.

hierarchy (HYE-ur-ahr-kee): A hierarchy is a system in which people are ranked above or below each other. The U.S. military has a hierarchy.

hypocrisy (hi-PAH-kri-see): Hypocrisy is behavior that does not align with what someone claims to believe. When the U.S. government fought for democracy abroad but did not allow rights to black Americans, it was hypocrisy.

segregate (SEG-ri-gate): To segregate is to keep groups of people separate. Wilson agreed to segregate black and white soldiers.

shrapnel (SHRAP-nul): Shrapnel includes bullets or pieces of shells. Some weapons sent shrapnel flying when they exploded.

SOURCE NOTES

1. "Woodrow Wilson's 'War Message to Congress.'" *Heritage Foundation*. Heritage Foundation, 2016. Web. 10 Aug. 2016.

2. Henry Louis Gates Jr. "Who Were the Harlem Hellfighters?" *Root*. Univision Communications, 11 Nov. 2013. Web. 10 Aug. 2016.

3. Jackson Stakeman and Randy Stakeman. "The NAACP and World War I." *Walter White Project*. Walter White Project, 17 Jun. 2012. Web. 10 Aug. 2016.

4. Henry Louis Gates Jr. "Who Were the Harlem Hellfighters?" *Root*. Univision Communications, 11 Nov. 2013. Web. 10 Aug. 2016.

5. "The Harlem Hellfighters and Henry Johnson Fighting in WWI." *For Love of Liberty*. For Love of Liberty, n.d. Web. 10 Aug. 2016.

6. Rebecca Onion. "A WWI-Era Memo Asking French Officers to Practice Jim Crow with Black American Troops." *Slate*. Slate Group, n.d. Web. 10 Aug. 2016.

7. "The Harlem Hellfighters and Henry Johnson Fighting in WWI." *For Love of Liberty*. For Love of Liberty, n.d. Web. 10 Aug. 2016.

8. Ibid.

9. Gilbert King. "Remembering Henry Johnson, the Soldier Called 'Black Death.'" *Smithsonian*. Smithsonian Institution, 25 Oct. 2011. Web. 10 Aug. 2016.

10. Hansi Lo Wang. "The Harlem Hellfighters: Fighting Racism in the Trenches of WWI." *NPR*. National Public Radio, 1 Apr. 2014. Web. 10 Aug. 2016.

11. Jeffrey T. Sammons and John H. Morrow Jr. *Harlem's Rattlers and the Great War*. Lawrence, KS: UP of Kansas, 2014. Print. 349.

12. Ibid. 359.

13. Sarah Kaplan. "WWI 'Harlem Hellfighter,' Relegated by Racism, to Receive Medal of Honor." *Washington Post*. Washington Post, 15 May 2015. Web. 10 Aug. 2016.

TO LEARN MORE

Books

Adams, Simon. *World War I*. New York: DK, 2014.

Brooks, Max. *The Harlem Hellfighters*. New York: Broadway, 2014.

Lewis, J. Patrick. *Harlem Hellfighters*. Mankato, MN: Creative, 2014.

Web Sites

Visit our Web site for links about the Harlem Hellfighters:
childsworld.com/links

Note to Parents, Teachers, and Librarians: We routinely verify our Web links to make sure they are safe and active sites. So encourage your readers to check them out!

INDEX